Sirens in Her Belly

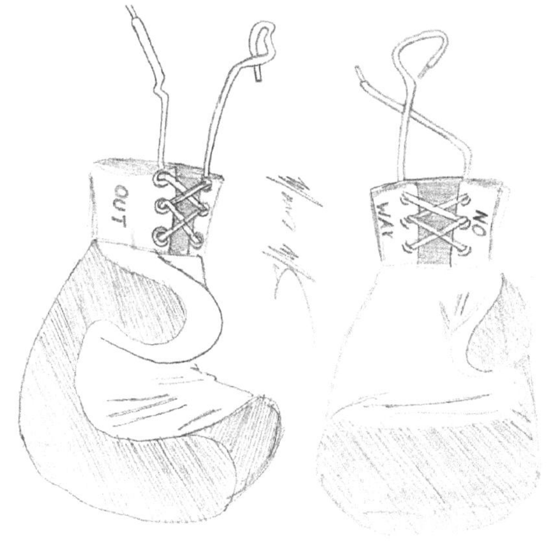

Copyright © 2015 Romaine Washington
ISBN: 978-0991297542
Published by Jamii Publishing
San Bernardino, CA
www.JamiiPublishing.com

All rights reserved. No part of this book may be reproduced, stored in a retrieval system, or transmitted in any form or by any means---electronic, mechanical, digital, photocopy, recording, or any other--- except for brief quotations in printed reviews, without the prior permission of the publisher.

DEDICATION

Thank you to my sons Marcus Muscato for your artwork and support, and Mitchell Washington for your pioneering spirit, and appreciation of poetry. I love you both. Thank you to my mother Betty L. Harden, father Major Mack L. Harden, and nephew William Harden.

Thank you to my friends: Darlene Coleman, Dr. Pamela Cotton-Roberts, Dr. Beverly Head, Chris Hollister, Intellectual Calibur, Stephanie Liggins, Sheila Louise Marchbanks, Richard May, Robin Paul, Mary Tawardos, Faye Vallone-Visconti and those who have supported and encouraged me on this writing journey.

Thank you to my childhood friend, Lamont and to those who stand up to bullies and protect those who would otherwise be victims.

Sirens in Her Belly

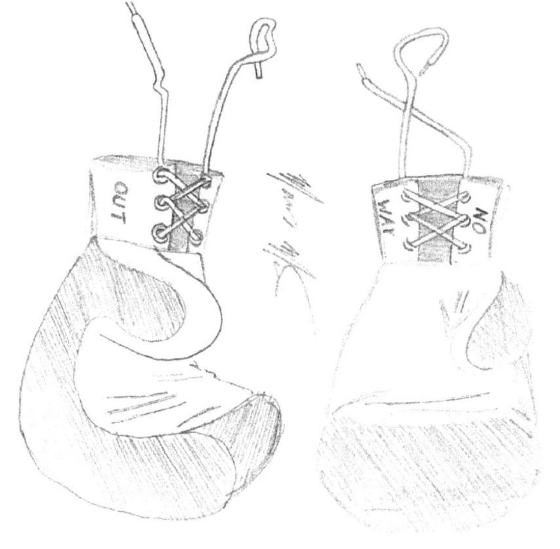

Romaine Washington

Table of Contents

Writers don't write from experience, although many are hesitant to admit that they don't... If you wrote from experience, you'd get one book, maybe three poems. Writers write from empathy.

– Nikki Giovanni

It Slipped Out

feet slap
floor afire
nowhere to run

from the disembodied tongue
and the sound of those words
twisted in a knotted fist

porcelain body
finely fired and cooled
silence trickling from eyes

impervious mirrors deflect
words like a current
returning to its source

we both gulp for air
flames and water
fight for flesh

we are searching for
sticks and stones
visible bruises or

a reason to explain this pain
words are too powerful
words are not powerful enough

Warning Shot

For Marissa Alexander, 2014

Each threat an
Ear drumming,
Menacing decree.
Wedged into
A sliver of sanity.
Adrenalin coursing
Through fingers.
Loaded and ready.
One more lie,
curse,
hit -
Will be the last.
Arrested for
Talking back,
Speaking out,
Shooting off
At the mouth,
Striking that
Impenetrable
Ceiling of death.
Resurrected
Villainous - victim
Battered - abuser.
Eyes bear down
The barrel of time.

The sun stands still.

In 2012, 31-year-old Marissa Alexander, former victim of domestic abuse, was sentenced to twenty years in prison for firing a warning shot in the ceiling to deter her ex-husband from escalating a conflict. No one was injured. Through public outcry, she was released from prison in January 2015. **(Joshua 10:12)**

Clemency

Words snarl,
Eat away at the floor
Like termites in heat.
Suck you in.
Condemned
Hope of being heard.
Squeezed inside
A chamber
Of desperation.
You shrink bullet-small
In lethal frustration.
Ceiling shot hole.
Stunned
One-eyed plaster
Stares at
So much noise
With no damage.

Reason shifts
Beneath feet.
Swallowed by
A sinkhole
Of injustice.
Bullet to bars
Warn us.
Outstretched
Arms ladder you
Up to justice.
Marissa,
Your name is
A rallying vigil
Against abuse.

Drowning
Object Lesson #2

i am his,
as sure as the hair on his head
the teeth in his mouth.

cared for, a little too much,
his teeth-flossed and brushed so intensely
they fall out seeking freedom.

cared for, a little too much,
like the hair in his comb
dead from exhaustion.

this is how it is with us.
a little too much for me
and not enough for him.

he looks for
a passing thought of lust
where he is not.

he reads my mail.
i watch him watch me
eyeballs to page.

better never leave me.
his hands collar my neck.
his body one long leash.

he pisses haloed circles around me.
wherever i go
i must carry his scent.

upon coming home
he sniffs me
with wolf-like skill.

his ghosted image
haunts the sound of air and shadow
as i stand naked.

my raped diaries lie exposed
graffitied by his red marker rage.
they blanket my bed.

i have forgotten
the pleasure
of quiet showers alone.

he permeates my pores.
i scrub myself raw
trying to find my scent.

i dissolve into hot water.
crushed rose-hips, steeped slowly,
i drown.

Fire and Sand

desert dirt clings to windpipes
surrounded by a circle of
full water glasses

simultaneously bursting.
the last glass breaks in his bare hands
by the weight of his laughter.

my chest constricts.
if i grovel on the floor for water,
will end up drinking my own blood.

if i walk away,
will need to dig shards
from my soles.

crying clears dust
from my throat.
i wake up thirsty again.

Object Lesson #1

the moment he sees her skin
the point
no longer   being human
she is black

a color to be used
sparingly –
if at all,

black –
a gaping hole of a tunnel,

black –
a night sky
in need of light,

black –
a color
he would rather not see.

he mimics
every gangsta rapper
known to mtv.
crosses his arms
this way and that,
with at-it-tude,
gives her
the 2-finger point –
says he's
mc poet – mc rap
mc yall
mc
she sees
al jolson
would be proud
of this performance.

One More Notch

Boy swaggers
Past the threshold of her door,
Pants loosely belted
Drooping on hip bones.
Before class is over
They will see what
He wears under.
An incidental shift or bend
Will reveal
The gap
In generations. Standard
Clothes fit around waist snug.
He wears loose gear
Drooping,
Begging to be seen
Like a lover half un-dressed
And always ready.
He saunters in,
Casually sits
Half boy/ half man
Strolling like he understands.
Why?
She asks him/he says,
It just feels right.
De-sign-er de times
Explains no-thing but
Un-heard herd mentality.
Her patience wanes
As gap waxes.
She orders him,
Pull up those pants.
He replies,
Why you even lookin' – cuz you know you like
What u c – I got it goin' on . . .
And so the line is drawn
Missed-respect/dis-understood
A tug o' war

Of belt straps and baggy attitudes.
She dreams designer pants
That would cover the gap
Between age and ageless,
A common core
Know-ledge
Is broad enough to make a difference.

What you lookin' at like dat?
He asks.
Your future, she replies – *if you*
Listen, I can show you
How to write that attitude
Into a flow
The whole world could read
Little seed – pull up them pants.

He smirks, *gangsta,*
Complies – pulls out paper
Borrows a pen for the hour,
Sits low-rider style
In a school-boy desk.
Belt moves one notch – gap closes
For the moment.

The lesson begins.

Dominant Trait

I
Blond-haired boy,
Fifteen,
Sits second seat
From front,
Faced-forward.
    He follows
    My every move,
    Like a laser
    On target.
Pupils a
White sheet
Reflection.
No mistaking
The narrow
Glared lens,
Rope-knotted
Gut
Tree
    Where he
    Carves
    My name.

II
Unnerved. I
    Peel details
To Mother's
    Stunned shame;
Speaks in
    Halting phrases
About his father -
    From Ozarks -
Conversations
    In the dark,
Passed down,
    Like a trade,

A tradition,
    A genetic trait,
She hoped
He would not
    Inherit.

III
Contorted scowl,
Blazing
Gnarled smile,
When he
Speaks.
    His father's
    Voice drowns
    The sound
    Of reason,
Lights
Flaming
Crossroads to
Manhood,
Where his
Son
Is centered.

Half of all hate crimes are committed by people between the ages of 15 and 24… directed against individuals and groups because of their race. There are 30 to 50 cross burnings a year. – FBI National Incident Based Reporting, 2014

Connoisseur

He says, ain't no more real Billie blues,
Jim Crow blues - lynchin' blues
Dyin' before livin' blues.

New blues is whinin' blues,
A pastel streak slapped against
The black and blue bruised blues.

Treble and bass lose the groveled groove
Of pain known from drug induced
Desperation seeking soothed reparation.

Kendrick and Badu blues lose
The brawling riffs amidst the moaning
Wail and pitch of hopelessness.

His comfortable steel blue eyes
Gauge the vintage quality of suffering.
A connoisseur of infliction only wants
The real thing.

Jazz

poets!
we too
            be jazz
musicians
            sassafrassan rhythm
improvisin' life
            and blowin'.
we too
            be rubato blue
Sachmo
            feelin'
Coltrane
            reelin'
    lovers.
and/syn
            co
pa
            tion
heavy down
            beat 6/8 time
waitin'
            tempo up
                        breathin' breezy easy
free
            we be
free
            we be
free
            we be
     jazz!

The Sound of Color

No color is mentioned
But you are colored
By tone and inflection
When they say
Your name / spit out
Like a wad of phlegm
Spewed hard and fast.
Each letter a hack of disgust
A parting of sound,
Southern drawl vowels
Against clipped dry consonants
And upturned lips.
Your name,
Coughed out each day as

I sit where you once sat.
I want to talk to you,
Gently whisper your name
In this room.
Say it how
It ought to be said.
Make it not sound
Like a disease,
A mistake,
A problem solved
With quotas and tokens.
I want to say it
How God says it each morning.
I want to say it
How I want my name to be said
When I am ghosted from this desk.
I want to say it
Until the cold white walls
Blossom brown warm bodies
Singing your name
In a Gregorian chant
Ave, brown girl, Ave.

Shaneika: Fleur de Soleil

She is the boldness
Of sunflowers and bumble bees,
Honey-toned, hand to hip,
Double-dutch tongue and sass
She sings her name,
Sha-neek-neek-ch-ch-ah-ah.

Shaneika
Is not shy/shallow/shadows
In the corner-quiet-coy.
She is the curve in hip,
Yellow in sun – shimmer in shine,
The flare at the tip – the dot of an i.
Her name is her song
Sung everyday
Just to remind us
Of the buzz of bees
And the surprise of sting,
Sha-neek-neek-ch-ch-ah-ah.

Big petaled flowers of sun
Are her crown,
Tall stalks of strength
Bend as she passes.
They wave in her honor
Sway in her rhythm
Grow in the reflection
Of joy that she is –
Shining / loud / bright / bold
Sunflower / bumble bee,
Sha-neek-neek-ch-ch-ah-ah.
Sha-neek-neek-ch-ch-ah-ah.
Don't ever stop
Don't ever stop
Don't ever stop
She-she-keep-on-keepin' on
She-she-keep-on-keepin'-on
Shaneika.

My Mother's Voice

My mother's voice
Is the soothe of lullabies
Cradled in midnight. And

My mother's voice
Is strong like Carmen McRae
When she speaks of flowers
She just doesn't waft in fragrance,
She goes to the root. And

My mother's voice
Is gospel,
Like Aretha before "Respect,"
And to the point – to the minute – TCB,
Aretha demanding R-E-S-P-E-C-T. And

My mother's voice
Is Harriet Tubman,
Hush-hush baby
Freedom is calling,
No more wailing on the other side.

Mahalia sings with my mother's voice, and
Maya speaks with my mother's voice, and
Nikki smiles at the sound of truth rippling through
Another year.

Sounds like wisdom,
        I thought I told you not to scoldings.
Sounds like hope,
        Go on baby you can do it.
Sounds like love,
        Everything is going to be all right.
Sounds just like – sounds just like
My mother's voice.

Diminutive

Don't let the photograph fool you.
This woman here
Can curse and kiss you at the same time.

Cool as the wisp of smoke
Ascending
From her cigarette,

Creates an angelic haze,
Softens disappointments around her eyes,
The veins like roots in her hands.

This woman is hard innocence,
Brazen Amazon of five-foot-two.
Those willowy arms can carry oak trees.

"She don't mean no harm," is often chanted
After she has stunned you into submission,
Collecting thoughts from scattered corners.

This one here can give you roses and thorns
At the same time, and you would
Bleed to death while intoxicated by the smell.

Don't let the photograph fool you.
A legion of witnesses can tell you,
This one is anything but small.

African Violets

Dedicated to Aunt Mary

From Tanzania

By the Lake that Thunders

They rise up from dark silt and

Suckled roots.

Purple velvet-petal tongues

Firmly planted in their

beauty.
They bathe in warm shadows

Beneath trees and shrubs

In umbrella-sun-shade.

Plucked up and transplanted,

African violets in American

soil.
Flowerpot secure,

On your windowsill they sit,

A precious bloom.

You tend the soft earth

Of the African violet

Because you understand

History to be a fragile thing,

Must be nurtured,

Requires a balance

Of light and shade.

Preservation

Depends on climate,

If left unattended

Will wither and die.

Dead.

You are gone now.

Tanzania has called you

home
And you leave a legacy

Of African violets

In bloom.

It's a Head Thang

He shears me
Like a work of art.
Layer
    By
         Layer,
             Buzzed
In freshly nibbled precision.
He sculpts my
             Knotty
Shafts of cheveux,
             Gently
Uncovering my soft spot
       In gris-gris strokes,
             Rearranges
Aura of my head
Strand
     By
        Strand.
             Weight
    Of old
         Growth falls
             Like
             Black
             Cotton
             Ball
             Tears
       In my
Leopard skin lap.
       He finds new root.
             Undresses
             My beauty
Nape to crown
                           And back again.
             He shears me
Like a work of art.

Myth and Mask

Myth: an idea that
is believed by many people,
but is not true.

Senegalese twists
Frame her face
Golden goddess,
Good she looks; but
Folks call her Medusa. So,
Some days, she is a goddess,
And some days –
A snake-headed monster,
But everyday
She wears
The myth and mask.
Woman wanting to be wholly beautiful.

Buzz-cut, sculpted scalp-tight
Can feel sun rays,
Wind tickle across her crown,
Queen of purse and time,
Lookin' fine; but
From atop her neck -
Misread. Men long
To turn her. Women
Approach – rejected.
Every day she wears
The myth and mask.
Woman wanting to be wholly beautiful.

Flowing braids,
Roots bound deep
As baobab trees, skyward,
Ancestral. Weaving
Fingers and time
Ticks long sitting.
Scalp tight, sleepless
Week in pain. Loose
Braids fray. Barren
Edges mark

Days she wears
The myth and mask.
Woman wanting to be wholly beautiful.

Pressed, to give it a rest,
Cute. Corporate
Nods of approval.
Lasts a short while.
Sweaty, singed heat,
Kinks creep beneath
Straight coif.
Sewn synthetic strands
Maintain 'do
For a season; but,
Poets' glare.
Claim she is unaware
Of her natural beauty.
Fake, phony and confused
She is accused
Of being a hair hypocrite.
She wears
The myth and mask.
Woman wanting to be wholly beautiful.

Dyed die of lye lies
Youthful kaleidoscope:
Chestnut- hazel- copper-rust-platinum-blush
Ginger-cinnamon-rose-flaming-obsidian-pitch
Teases eyes,
Disguises time in a myriad
Of guesses.
She smiles
Playful. Ends split.
Fragments
Pop and drift.
Shedding shafts.
Brittle bottle bursts
Ashen grey.
She wears
The myth and mask.

Woman wanting to be wholly beautiful.

Her hair is knot, she
Is not, sham of shame,
She does not wear.
Whole and beautiful as she is.
Locked-Twisted
Buzzed- braided
Weaved-straightened
Are options,
Not a political statement
Of who she is,
Where she's been,
Where she's goin'.
Intertwined with time,
The receding line of life
Curls about us all.

Unsung

Pots and pans
Knock air into meat
Of pounding muscle.

A fist of yawn
Engulfs mouth.
There is no speaking

To a morning
That otherwise
Marches on.

Steps are
Bone on bone
Battered.

Hope wedged in hips.
Backbone crumbles
Beneath the weight

Of wait.
Gravity and ashes
Melt into hair.

Severed Hands

Lacquered black hair
Frames high-cheek-boned
Peach-colored face.
Full, square jaw
Equaled by broad shoulders
Quietly sturdy, she sits with

A lapful of watercolor markers
Still warm
From friendly notes.
No one knows
The hands that use these markers
Bleed lonely red-wrist-tears.
Wrapped in
Gauze and Prozac trust,

Life sometimes
Is a cruel-edged-razor
Whose pain can slit
The thickest skin.

Scientist say,
When we are born
We die
Without touch.

My palms are weeping.
Her shame is my guilt
Of not knowing how to be more.
Hope is seeing her face
Just one more day
And one more day again.

As her severed hands draw,
My severed hands write.

Touch is a matter of perception.
Her presence touches me

Sirens in Her Belly

For Tanisha
Anderson, (1977-2014)

You are in my mirror
When I wake.
        There is no
        Shaking the brute hands
        And bullet knees
        Crushing you lifeless.
Windowed eyes of
Mother-brother-daughter
Helplessly watch.
Want to stop -
Before you are
        Bulldozed into backseat;
        Like a criminal
        Who has robbed a bank,
        Stabbed a stranger,
        Kidnapped a child,
        Molested.
Want to stop them
From molesting your mind
Already troubled
With visions
No one else can see.

You are more
Than stats
Of mental illness
        Murdered;
More than
A handful of memories
        Trickling down
        The sides of pain,
Swallowed by
A vortex of voices
Trying to forget.
No national rally cry
Of hoodies, hands up,

Or *Black Lives Matter,*

When you are a woman.
No marching outcry.
Though animals
Have purple-black-and brindle
Ribbons
    To protect from
    Cruel, inhumane.
There is no ribbon
For this tragedy.

You live a different reality,
Have a lime-green ribbon
    Squeezed into
    The meat of your brain.
A mind folding in on itself
Like a newspaper
Neatly tucked away;
    Indelible print
    Rubs into my fingertips.
I touch your story - daily,
Your pet pit bull, Drama,
Your journalism dreams,
Your anti-drug slogan.
The normalcy
Of moment-by-moment.
    Want to resurrect you.
    This blaring sorrow
    Cries out for justice.
Sirens in your belly
  Wail and...

In 2014, 37-year-old Tanisha Anderson was killed by police when the family called to have her mentally evaluated for erratic behavior - *The Guardian* by Michelle Dean.
July 4, 2015 Washington Post: at least 125 people, identified by family or the police as mentally ill have died during police encounters.
Note: Lime-green commemorative ribbon represents mental illness.

Birth of the Blues

Genesis 4: 1-15

At open casket
Eve is baptized
In blood soaked moans.

She wails wildly for her sons
Both banished from her arms.

There is no fruit sweet enough
To heal the bitterness.
Adam is silent - Eve is empty.

The snake
Slithers over newspaper print.

There are bullet holes where eyes used to be.
Eve weeps relentless
Waiting for us to join her.

Profile August, 1965

Top insurance sales woman, coiffed.
Red pumps with lipstick to match.
She does not gun the engine,
But drives with bullet speed
In her pearl-white, tail-finned, Cadillac.

Sweat and gasoline perfumes the air.
Time explodes like a meteor,
A burst of brilliance drifting into a whimper.
The bashing of heads.

Burn-baby-burn
Flashes like the sheen of her red pumps.
Burn-baby-burn
Races with the fury of a caddy down our dead end street.
Burn-baby burn

Into the retina of my heart,
Black and White riot flames
Across our TV

As mom puffs on cigarettes
Smoke bathes her hair –
Ashes weep in trays about the house
We dare not leave.

I will never be
Only a little girl again.
Innocence is a place,
Burning and ravaged.

Watts riots began with a traffic incident, August 11th however, the reasons for the riots were rooted in unwritten discriminatory hiring practices, unfair housing, cross burnings and police harassment…

We Need Video Cam Eyes

For Rodney King

(1965-2012)

Rodney
Today I saw 2 cop cars
Pull over
A Latino man
In a powder blue '65 Chevy.
I cried out
To the man pulled over,
Are you o.k. brother?
                Are you o.k.?
Once I would have wondered
What he'd done,
        But now
        After seeing you beaten
        A ragdoll effigy,
Two cities
From where I live,
A breath and
Minute away
From my arm chair
And video cam eyes…
        I watch you shrivel up
        Blood heap moan.
                Fractured skull,
                Brains spilling out
                On policeman's shoes.
        I watch you writhe
        Like a South
        African sacrifice;
You are here
Inside of me,
Rolling through
Shattered replay
Of safety

Poised, peering,
Video cam eyes

That could not
Help then,
Help now.
They flesh and bone
An enemy,
Who would otherwise
Be a ghost.
You would otherwise
Be another nigger
In the wilderness
Echoing brutality.
To hollow ears.
Even with cameras rolling
Police sought alibis
And justifications,
But found none
As solid
As a swift kick in the gut,
But found none
To avert
The bludgeoned truth.

We tremble,
Pinned down like you,
Sprawled in blood
Blow by blow

With each repeated broadcast
Beaten blue bruised
With each repeated broadcast
In black and white
With each repeated broad cast
With each repeated broadcast
With each repeated broadcast

The acquittal of the four police officers involved in the beating was the catalyst for the 1992 uprising in Los Angeles where there were 53 deaths and over 11,000 arrests and over 2,000 injuries reported.

Exonerated: A Crucifixion

For Kalief Browder

(1993-2015)
Prison guard batons
Turn his pulsing brain
To crumbling brick,
Razor thin cracks of
Uncontrollable impulse.
                    Blind-eye-witness
                    Shackles his freedom
Slice by slice
He stares, blank hands
And empty lips
Peeling oranges
Already devoured.
                    No money.
                    No bail.
His lamb tongue
On the roof
Of his mouth
Gnaws away
At the slices of thought
That dribble down
The back of his throat.
                    Amendment Thirteen
                    Revoked,
                    Counting backwards
                    Eight-Six-Five-Four
Morsels of memories spew
Bones rattling down corridors,
Into solitary corners
Filled with elbows and toes,
Shavings of nails.
                    Gangs replace
                    Bare back
                    Overseer beatings.
His eyes bleed
Seeds and pulp,
Squeezed dry

Hallucinations form
Brick walls
Crushing towards him.

Puss oozing welts
Raise a battered map
A thousand days and
Two centuries in the making.

Orange prison jumpsuits
Pummel his innocence.
Sheared and deboned by
Judges with razor gavels.

Time served
For no crime.
Charges dropped
With no trial.

This nightmare is a lie.
This nightmare is living.
This nightmare will not die.
This nightmare
Is in the orange brick sheets
He slices and carves with
Razors of waking howls.

Sixteen-year-old Kalief Browder was charged with robbery and arrested. The items were never recovered. Browder spent three years in Rikers where the case never came to trial. June 2013, he was released without explanation. June 2015 he committed suicide.

Strange Fruit: A Communion

Poplar cells in *Strange Fruit*/ vale.
Familiar tracks.
Cement swallows
Unarmed Oak-
Land blood
Of a million feet.
Father - daughter
Dances die
This New Year's night.
Knee crushing head,
Bullet in back.
We die with
Oscar Grant. Ashe
Hoodied in de hood of
Night. Armed with
Arizona and Skittles.
Slender, tender teen,
Suspiciously walks
Alone.
Talks to friend on
Cell phone.
Stalked
by Zimmer-
Man standing
His ground
Beneath *southern trees.*
Villainized victim.
Verdict issued
Bullet of
Unavenged Death.
We die with
Trayvon Martin. Ashe

Gas station – carload SUV
In passenger seat
He bops to
Bass beatin' windows

Bouncin'. Hands wavin'
Celebratin' being alive.
Dunn disturbed,
By de music. Dis-
Charges his opinion
With bullet precision. Unarmed
Murder in the *southern breeze.*
We die with
Jordan Davis. Ashe
Backpack-less in Bronx
On his way home.
High school sophomore,
Unarmed. Unaware -
Accusations can be lethal.
Without evidence,
Riker's becomes
Guantanamo Bay.
A political prisoner of poverty
Has no right to a speedy trial.
The bulging eyes and
Twisted mouth hang.
In PTSD suicide.
We die with
Kalief Browder. Ashe
Hands up. Too many
To count. A strange and
Bitter unarmed crop
Of young black boys and
Men. Too many to name.
We die
With you. Waiting
For resurrection. Ashe

Oscar Grant (1986 – Jan. 1, 2009) 23; Trayvon Martin (1995- Feb. 26, 2012) 17; Jordan Davis III (1995 – Nov. 23, 2012) 17; Kalief Browder (1993-June 6, 2015) 22. Ashe: Refers to the spiritual life force that flows through things, much like the Chinese concept of chi. Ashe is also a way of saying, "so let it be", and can also be "amen" as used by Christians following a prayer.

Asphyxiation – Prison Poem #1

the absence of air
vacuumed through veins,

chest heaves out of habit.

asthmatic lungs rasp
slowly brain dulls.

your mouth moves
charades in clueless form.

my imagination cannot bare
the chaos of you in an inverted world.

where there is no gravity,
only chains, bars, numbers.

collect calls
through hurricane phone connections.

asthmatic, I
gasp for what is not there.

my hand juts weightless through the phone
searching oxygen and you.

First Code of a Dragon Slayer

You come
Roarin'
Machete breath
Threats,
As though I have never been
Pierced before,
As though my skin
Weren't scarred over
So many times
I am platinum
Body armor,
As though I have never been
Beheaded before,
Mind severed,
Projectile thoughts cursing
In volcanic devastation.
Hydra is now my name.
Got so many heads,
Each time you come
At me
I grow stronger,
Out think
Your tired tactics
Of subjugation.
Your tantrum wielding
Methods of manipulation
Are but clipped claws
Beneath my feet.

You puff
Your prison
Tatted chest out
As though size, or legend,
Are points of power.
You are a pin
Prick of truth
Away from deflation.

No one
Respects your methods
Of intimidation.
Bars don't make you
More fierce,
Crazy,
Or dangerous.
Draggin' that dragon
Reputation
Into this fight
Don't mean you win.

Your desperate
Claims of annihilation
Feed me
Determination
To stand my ground,
Firm-
Small-
Impervious.
The very thing
You want
You can-
Not have.
Cannot
Feed on
Fear from me
To enhance
Your illusion
Of potency.
I see you
For the monster
You are.

Your hate
Is a boomerang
Eating you
Inside out.

Treadmill

Running on the foot-
Ball field, through
Airports-Benson Hurst
L.A. to Orange County and back.
Running back/ back running
Like a runaway slave,
Like Bigger Thomas
After he killed Mary Dalton.
                Cremated phoenix,
                Fifty years later
                Nicole rises from the ashes
                As Bessie waits for eulogy.

We watched you
Turn to feathers flapping
Like you had a goal,
A touchdown,
A plane to catch,
A car to rent,
A woman to love.
Flying like you were a bird.
We watched you
Hang glide for the Bills,
Hertz, and Honey glazed.
Running.

You were teeing up green,
Club shining,
Teeth grinning,
As though you were
        Running to
                Instead of
                        Running from.

The Boy Next Door

We run like two bunnies
In an open field
Chasing fairy wishes,
Fuzzy angel-hair balls floating
Slightly out of grasp.
Disappointment comes
In the cup of empty fists.
You kiss my palm,
Call me "cuz,"
As we make plans to try again.

You and me Bruce Lee
Wooden boards
Between two bricks.
We chop our hands
Juicy bruised,
Steak-red-tender.
Pretend it don't hurt.
But find some/anything else to do.

We sneak Oreos and Kool-aid,
Eat the middle first,
White icing coats our teeth,
Followed by black cookie,
Washed down by red-sugar-water.
We mainline our summers
In a rush of sweet
110 degrees of sun
Toasting us like Oreo crusts.

To cool down,
We water the garden.
Slip off our shoes,
We being the most important plants,
H2o-ooh in arched back giggles -
As cool in mud in shade we play.

...and here comes the
Up-the-street bully
Wanting to pick at me
Because he is bored
And I am here.
You say - don't touch her man -
"She my cuz."
As big as Goliath you stand,
Your words alone
Knock the thought
Out his head.
I stand next to you,
Unrelated
But by the blood
Transfusion
Of your words,
"She my cuz."
Unrelated,
Except for the kiss in palm,
Water down spine,
Sugar-coated mouth,
Bruised-hand chops,
And words that stop
A bully in his thoughts.

We didn't know it then, but
This was our summer
Of perfect innocence.
And that day
Has been snap shot
Into the photo album
Memory of my mind,
Goliath tall and gallantly kind.
And when my sistah friends complain
There ain't no good men,
I think of you – I think of you - and smile.

A Tribute to Spike Lee (circa 1992)

Radio spills saxophone
Sounds through open windows,
Breeze swirls,
Music
   Summersaults
Into a surreal fingerpopping frenzy.
   Rise alto lithe and lyrical, solo
A chant,
Just a whisper of a chant,
   A love supreme – a love supreme.
This is one of those days
   A love supreme
To write a poem,
   A love supreme
Watch a movie,
   A love supreme
Be a movie.
   A love supreme
Stepping into
   School Daze
Steppin.'
Surrounded by Jigaboos and Wannabees.
Sister Joie full of sass.
Eric splashing sepia everywhere.
Blanchard in the background,
While the drums of
   Jungle Fever
Pa-pound pa-pound pa-pound-ing
On my brown skin.
This is the kind of day
Too beautiful not to birth a revolution.

At any given moment
Mookie, Cyrus, Shorty
Giant, Half-Pint, Mars Blackman,
Spike Lee
Could split the screen wide open.

Just slice it with a tongue of truth,
Expose unwanted battles,
Dialogue,
Talk about – talk about
What we would not.

Do ya know – do ya know – do ya know

At any given moment
All this perfect quiet
Over color
Could erupt into the rage
That pushes the day forward.
Do ya know-do ya know – do ya know
At any given moment
        A Love supreme
Could decide to
        Do the Right Thing

Give accolades to
        Mo' Better Blues.
At any given time
"By any means necessary"
40 acres and a mule could
        Malcolm X
It's way to the Academy door;
Drive Miss Daisy to the curb.

"Please baby baby baby please
Baby please please please" -
I gotta have it
        A love supreme
He's gotta have it
        A love supreme
She's Gotta Have It
        A love supreme
A love supreme

Thank You Spike Lee

Sacrament

Roosevelt
Sells fresh fruit
On the corner,
Wears a suit and bowtie
Straight lines - no creases
90 degree summer
20 degree winter he sells pies.

Roosevelt
Is there
As sure as
The stoplight.
Each morning drive by
To see his stark white shirt and teeth
Like clouds in sky
Invite me to gaze and dream.
His eyes a hello of good morning.
I must brake
Even against the green
Go of traffic.

"How much" – I ask,
His hands full of ripe garden grown,
"2 dollars" - he dangles
Breakfast before me and
I feel as though we are
Adam and Eve and
This is every good tree
Right here on this corner,
Roosevelt is good and
I am good.
God is good.
The fruit is good.

The homeless
Are waking from their benches.
I can hear the cry of rusted

Shopping carts.
As though I were throwing
Money in a wishing well,
I tell Roosevelt
To feed someone who needs it.
He says
"I always do,"
Thrusts an armful in my car,
Serious
Smile unchanged.
No words
But his eyes say
"Take - eat
It has been given up
For you."

I bow my head
And drive away . . .

ACKNOWLEDGEMENTS

The following poems in this collection previously appeared, in one form or another, in the following publications:

Clemency - *Stand Our Ground*: Anthology for Trayvon Martin and Marissa Alexander. **Diminutive** - *Number One*. **Drowning** - *Lullwater Review*. **Jazz**: *Phineas*, *Marsha Harden. *Blue Milk*. *Buckle &*. **Object Lesson #1** - *The Black Scholar Journal*. **One More Notch** - *Defining Moments*: Anthology of Teachers' Writing. Plymouth Writer's Group. *California English*: A Home for Hip Hop. **We Need Video Cam Eyes** – *The Verdict Is In*: Anthology on the 1992 L.A. Uprising, *Marsha Muscato. **The Boy Next Door** & **A Tribute to Spike Lee** – *Brothers and Others*: Anthology of Black women writing about Black men.

*indicates alternate name the poem was published under.

Strange Fruit: A Communion uses lyrics from the song *Strange Fruit*, written by Abel Meeropol and recorded by Billie Holiday, 1939.

ABOUT THE AUTHOR

Romaine Washington is a native Californian whose poetry has been published in *Stand Our Ground: Anthology for Trayvon Martin and Marissa Alexander*, *Defining Moment: Anthology of Teachers' Writing*, *Brothers & Others: Anthology of Black Women Writing About Black Men*, *The Verdict is In: Anthology on the L.A. Uprising*, *Lullwater Review Emory University*, *California English: A Home for Hip-Hop*, *The Black Scholar*, *New Directions: Howard University*, *Number One*, *San Fernando Poetry Journal*, *Blue Milk: Art Periodical*, *Buckle &*, *Phineas*. She has a chapbook *Coffeehouse Chatter* published by Red Dancefloor Press.

From California to Georgia, from high schools and college classrooms, to churches and coffeehouses, Romaine has been a featured poet in a wide variety of venues. Previously, she was a member of a Georgia Slam team that competed in Ann Arbor, Michigan and was one of four finalist. In addition to live featured performances she has also presented her poetry on community television programs in Georgia and on a variety of radio programs from National Public Radio (NPR) to KPFK Los Angeles, KUCB Santa Barbara, WRFG and WAOK in Atlanta, Georgia. Romaine is an active member in the California poetry community. She participates as a feature in open mics, as well as poetry workshops.

A fellow of the Inland Area Writing Project (IAWP) University California Riverside (UCR), Romaine served as poet-in-resident at the Riverside Mission Inn for three years. In IAWP, she has also been a presenter and facilitator in the Summer Writing Program on the UCR campus, and was also a presenter for a Pre-CATE (California Teachers of English) conference.

Romaine is a graduate of Azusa Pacific University with a Master in Education and a Bachelor of Arts in French from California State University San Bernardino. She is a public high school teacher in California. To foster a love and appreciation of poetry in her students she invites poets and spoken word artists to perform in her classroom and on campus. Her students are also encouraged to attend and participate in local college and community poetry readings.

Something Bigger Than This

Out of all the ideas

Man has created: Fate
By far is the cruelest

Stalking life into a box of
Mystery,
It waits to devour your existence;
Life a cobweb
To an insect

Fate is a concept that lingers everywhere
Making life as fragile as a wish

Mitchell Washington

CPSIA information can be obtained
at www.ICGtesting.com
Printed in the USA
LVHW052054170122
708712LV00007B/157